LA LUPA

for Nick Starr

THE ROYAL SHAKESPEARE COMPANY

The Royal Shakespeare Company is probably one of the best-known theatre companies in the world. It has operated in its present form since 1961 when it changed its name from the Shakespeare Memorial Theatre Company, established a London base and widened its repertoire to embrace works other than Shakespeare.

Today the RSC has five home theatres. In Stratford the Royal Shakespeare Theatre stages large-scale productions of Shakespeare's plays; the Swan, a galleried Jacobean playhouse, brings to light the plays of many of his neglected contemporaries alongside classics of world theatre, while The Other Place, the company's studio theatre, houses some of the company's most exciting experimental and contemporary work, as well as providing a regular venue for visiting companies and some of the RSC's education work, including the annual Prince of Wales Shakespeare School.

In 1982 the company moved its London home to the Barbican Centre, where in the large-scale Barbican Theatre and the studio-sized Pit, the company stages work transferring from Stratford as well as new productions.

But Stratford and London are only part of the story. Recent years have seen a dramatic increase in the reach of the RSC, with major RSC productions on tour around the UK and abroad, in addition to the company's annual resident seasons in Newcastle upon Tyne and Plymouth. Productions from Stratford and London visit regional theatres, while our annual regional tour continues to set up its own travelling auditorium in schools and community centres around the country. This ensures that the RSC's productions are available to the widest possible number of people geographically. A lively programme of education work accompanies all this work, creating the audiences of tomorrow by bringing the excitement and the power of theatre to young people all over the country.

In the past few years the company has also taken Shakespeare to enthusiastic audiences in Europe, the USA, Australia, New Zealand, South America, Japan, India and Pakistan, and this year the company will visit Hong Kong, Spain, Turkey and Korea. The RSC is grateful to The British Council for its support of its overseas touring programme.

Despite enormous changes over the years, the company today is still formed around a core of associate actors and actresses, whose artistic talents combine with those of the world's top directors and designers and the most highly-skilled technical workshops to give a distinctive and unmistakable approach to theatre. The play you are seeing tonight is at once a link in a great tradition and a unique event.

THE ROYAL SHAKESPEARE COMPANY

RSC EDUCATION

The objective of the RSC Education Department is to enable as many people as possible from all walks of life to have easy access to the great works of Shakespeare, the Renaissance and the Theatre.

To do this, we are building a team which supports the productions that the company presents onstage for the general public, special interest groups and education establishments of all kinds.

We are also planning to develop our contribution as a significant learning resource in the fields of Shakespeare, the Renaissance, classical and modern theatre, theatre arts and the RSC. This resource is made available in many different ways, including workshops, teachers' programmes, summer courses, a menu of activities offered to group members of the audience, pre- and post-show events as part of the Events programme, open days, tours of the theatre, community activities, youth programmes, loans of parts of the RSC Collection for exhibitions etc.

We are building, for use world wide, a new web site to be launched this year. This will make available all of the above, as well as providing access to the RSC's collection of historic theatre and Shakespearean material. It will also carry interesting and interactive material about the work of the RSC.

We can also use our knowledge of theatre techniques to help in other aspects of learning: classroom teaching techniques for subjects other than drama or English, including management and personnel issues.

Not all of these programmes are available all the time, and not all of them are yet in place. However, if you are interested in pursuing any of these options, the telephone numbers and e-mail addresses are as follows:

For information on general education activities, contact Education Administrator Sarah Keevill on 01789 403462, or e-mail her on sarah.keevill@rsc.org.uk.

To find out about backstage tours, please contact our Tour Manager Anne Tippett on 01789 403405, or e-mail her on theatre.tours@rsc.org.uk.

JOIN THE RSC

For £8 a year you can join the RSC's Mailing List as an Associate member. Regular mailings will bring you:

* Advance information and priority booking for RSC seasons in Stratford, London, Newcastle and Plymouth

* Deferred payment facilities for the London Season and the Stratford Summer Festival Season 2000 when tickets are paid for by credit card

* Seasonal offers on the Stratford StopOver scheme

* Special members' events in Stratford and London

* Details of UK and overseas touring and information about RSC transfers to the West End.

* Free RSC Magazine

* No fees payable on ticket re-sales in Stratford.

* Full membership at £24, social groups at £10 and education groups at £8 give even more benefits

Overseas Members. The RSC tours regularly overseas. Wherever you are in the world, you can be a member of the RSC's mailing List. Overseas Membership is available from £15.

STAY IN TOUCH

For up-to-date news on the RSC, our productions and education work, visit the RSC's official web site: **www.rsc.org.uk**. Further information on the RSC is also available on Teletext.

A PARTNERSHIP WITH THE RSC

The RSC is immensely grateful for the valuable support of its corporate sponsors and individual and charitable donors. Between them these groups provide over £6m a year for the RSC and support a range of initiatives such as actor training, education workshops and access to our performances for all members of society.

Amongst our corporate sponsors, we are especially grateful to Allied Domecq, principal sponsor since 1994, for its far-sighted and long-standing relationship. Allied Domecq's announcement that its principal sponsorship will come to a natural end in 2001 provides an exciting opportunity for companies to form new corporate partnerships with the RSC, as principal sponsor, as a member of the RSC's new Business Partners programme or as a corporate member.

As an individual you may wish to support the work of the RSC through membership of the RSC Patrons. For as little as £21 per month you can join a cast drawn from our audience and the worlds of theatre, film, politics and business. Alternatively, the gift of a legacy to the RSC would enable the Company to maintain and increase new artistic and educational work with children and adults through the Acting and Education Funds.

For information about corporate partnership with the RSC, please contact:
Robert Fleming
Head of Sponsorship Development
Barbican Theatre, London EC2Y 8BQ
Tel: 020 7382 7139
E-mail: robert.fleming@rsc.org.uk

For information about individual relationships with the RSC, please contact:
Graeme Williamson
Development Manager
Royal Shakespeare Theatre, Waterside
Stratford-upon-Avon CV37 6BB
Tel: 01789 412661
E-mail: graemew@rsc.org.uk

You can visit our web site at **www.rsc.org.uk/development**

GIOVANNI VERGA - Some background material

With his tightly-knit prose, his immediacy and directness, his powerful conciseness, and his lyricism, Verga was ahead of his time...The only work of his that became widely known was *Cavalleria rusticana*, thanks to the theatre version and to Mascagni's opera. Fame was to come to Verga after World War 1, when readers and critics finally realized his greatness. Since then he has been a profound influence on contemporary Italian literature. This should not be surprising, for most of the narrative devices of twentieth-century fiction were already his.

(Giovanni Cecchetti, Professor of Italian at UCLA and translator of several of Verga's works)

*

Giovanni Verga (1840-1922)

1840 Born 2 September in Catania, Sicily.

1850 Attends one of the island's few non-church schools, where he studies Italian literature and is encouraged to become a writer.

1859 Enrols in the Law Faculty at Catania University but soon loses interest and devotes himself instead to writing.

1862 Leaving the university, he uses the remainder of his fees to finance the publication of *I carbonari della montagna* (The Mountain Carbonari), a historical and patriotic novel.

1863 *Sulle lagune* (On the Lagoon) published in 4 parts in a Florence newspaper, a major step forward.

1865 Leaves Sicily for the first time to visit Florence, then the cultural capital of Italy, which over the next few years is to become his second home. A personable and attractive young man, he is popular in society and is taken up by the literati as a writer of great promise. The Florence period produces *Una peccatrice* (A Sinner), the more important *Storia di una capinera* (The Blackcap's Story) and a play *Rose caduche* (Fallen Roses). These, like much of Verga's early writing, are characterised by sensuality and an over-heated eroticism.

1872 Leaves Florence for Milan, returning regularly to Catania. Publishes the novel *Eva*.

1874 After *Eros* and *Tigre real* (Royal Tigress) comes a completely new departure, the novella *Nedda, a sketch from Sicily*, his first work with a Sicilian rural setting in which he begins to use naturalistic dialogue suited to the location. This is a turning point in Verga's work, showing him strongly influenced by French realist writers like Zola and Flaubert.

1880 Beginning of Verga's mature period in which he finds his true voice. Publishes *Vita dei Campi* (Life in the Fields), a collection of short Sicilian stories which includes 'La Lupa' and 'Cavalleria rusticana'.

1881 Begins the planned five-volume 'Cycle of the Doomed', charting the fortunes of a Sicilian family through several generations. Only the first two books, *I Malavoglia* (published in English as The House by the Medlar Tree) and *Mastro-Don Gesualdo* (1889) are completed.

1883 Publishes *Novelle rusticane*, a collection of stories, and re-works 'Cavalleria rusticana' into a one-act tragedy which proves a triumph on its premiere in Turin the following year. Verga is involved in scandal, enhancing his already-established reputation as a philanderer.

1890 Mascagni's opera *Cavalleria rusticana*, derived from Verga's story but by other librettists, is an enormous success. Owing to contractual disputes, however, Verga's role in the process is not recognised: his claim to a financial interest in the opera sparks long-running litigation.

1894 Verga returns to settle again in Catania but continues to visit the mainland frequently. The third volume of the Malavoglia saga, *Duchessa de Leyra*, is begun but abandoned. He enters a period of disappointment and bitterness, convinced that his work is no longer well regarded.

1896 After Puccini abandons plans for an opera based on 'La Lupa', Verga re-works the story into a two-act play which is staged at Turin. Its lukewarm reception is a further source of disappointment to Verga.

1901 Two plays, *La caccia al lupo* (The Wolf Hunt) and *La caccia alla volpe* (The Fox Hunt) staged in Milan.

1905 His last work, *Dal tuo al mio* (From Yours to Mine) published as a novella: the previous year a dramatic version had been performed in Rome.

1912 The film industry's interest in some of his stories briefly engages Verga's attention but generally he maintains a dignified silence and acknowledges himself forgotten.

1919 Publication of Luigi Russo's first full critical evaluation revives interest in Verga's work.

1920 Luigi Pirandello presides at a meeting in Rome to honour Verga's 80th birthday: when celebrations are planned later in Catania, Verga refuses to attend the ceremony, maintaining that they have 'left it too late'. In October the state honours him by appointing him Senator of the Kingdom of Italy.

1922 Verga dies.

*

Verga's style: *Verismo*

'I had published some of my first novels. They went well. I was preparing others. One day, I don't know how, there came into my hands a sort of broadside, a halfpenny sheet, sufficiently ungrammatical and disconnected, in which a sea captain succinctly related all the vicissitudes through which his sailing-ship had passed. Seaman's language, short, without an unnecessary phrase. It struck me and I read it again, it was just what I was looking for, without definitely knowing it. Sometimes, you know, just a sign, an indication is enough. It is a revelation...'

(Verga in DH Lawrence's translation)

*

DH Lawrence was one of the first British writers to appreciate Verga's work. He translated the novel *Mastro-Don Gesualdo* and *'Cavalleria rusticana' and other stories*, in which the prose version of 'La Lupa' first appeared. Lawrence's Introductions to his editions have much to say about Verga's work and the background to his stories.

From the Introduction to *'Cavalleria rusticana' and other stories*

The family of the future author lived chiefly at Catania, the seaport of east Sicily, under Etna. And Catania was really Verga's home town, just as Vizzini was his home village.

But as a young man of twenty, he already wanted to depart into the bigger world of 'the Continent', as the Sicilians called the mainland of Italy. It was the Italy of 1860, the Italy of Garibaldi, and the new era. Verga seems to have taken little interest in politics. He had no doubt the southern idea of himself as a gentleman and an aristocrat, beyond politics. And he had the ancient southern thirst for show, for lustre, for glory, a desire to figure grandly among the first society of the world. His nature was proud and unmixable. At the same time, he had the southern passionate yearning for tenderness and generosity. And so he ventured into the world, without much money; and in true southern fashion, he was dazzled...He was a handsome man, by instinct haughty and reserved...For nearly twenty years he lived in Milan, in Florence, in Naples, writing and imagining he was fulfilling his thirst for glory by having love affairs with elegant ladies: most elegant ladies, as he assures us...

Then, toward the age of forty, came the recoil, and the Cavalleria rusticana volume is the first book of the recoil. It was a recoil away from the *beau monde* and the 'Continent', back to Sicily, to Catania, to the peasants...He had to go to Vizzini and more or less manage the farm work - at least keep an eye on it. He said he hated the job, that he had no capacity for business, and so on. But we may be sure he managed very well. And certainly from this experience he gained his real fortune, his genuine sympathy with peasant life, instead of his spurious sympathy with elegant ladies. His great books all followed: *Cavalleria rusticana* and *Mastro-Don Gesualdo* and the *Novelle rusticane* and most of the sketches have their scenes laid in or around Vizzini...

In *Cavalleria rusticana*, however, Verga had not yet come to the point of letting loose his pity. He is still too much and too profoundly offended, as a passionate male... When one reads, one after the other, the stories of Turiddu, La Lupa, Jeli, Brothpot, Rosso Malpelo, stories of crude killing, it seems almost too much, too crude, too violent, too much a question of mere brutes. As a matter of fact, the judgement is unjust. Turiddu is not a brute, neither is Alfio. Both are men of sensitive and even honourable nature...As for Jeli, who could call him a brute? or Nanni? They are perhaps not brutal enough. They are too gentle and forbearing, too delicately naïve... And so grosser natures trespass on them unpardonably; and the revenge flashes out...

What Verga's soul yearned for was the purely human being, in contrast to the sophisticated. It seems as if Sicily, in some way, under all her amazing forms of sophistication and corruption, still preserves some flower of pure human candour...

Verga turns to the peasants only to seek for something which, as a healthy artist, he worshipped. Even Tolstoy, as a healthy artist, worshipped it the same. It was only as a moralist and a personal being that Tolstoy was perverse. As a true artist he worshipped, as Verga did, every manifestation of pure, spontaneous, passionate life, life kindled to vividness... And these stories, instead of being out of date, just because the manners depicted are more or less obsolete, even in Sicily, which is a good deal Americanised and 'cleaned up', as the reformers would say; instead of being out of date, they are dynamically perhaps the most up-to-date of stories.

From the Introduction to *Mastro-Don Gesualdo*

The Sicilians of today are supposed to be the nearest thing to the classic Greeks that is left to us: that is, they are the nearest descendants on earth. In Greece today there are no Greeks. The nearest thing is a Sicilian, the eastern and south-eastern Sicilian...He has the energy, the quickness, the vividness of the Greek, the same vivid passion for wealth, the same ambition, the same lack of scruples, the same queer openness, without ever really openly committing himself. He is not a bit furtive, like an Italian. He is astute instead, far too astute and Greek to let himself be led by the nose. Yet he has a certain frankness, far more than an Italian. And far less fear than an Italian. His boldness and his daring are Sicilian rather than Italian, so is his independent manliness...

The people, too, have some of the old Greek singleness, carelessness, dauntlessness. It is only when they bunch together as citizens that they are squalid. In the countryside, they are portentous and subtle, like the wanderers in the *Odyssey*. And their relations are all curious and immediate, objective. They are so little aware of themselves, and so much aware of their own effects.

Acknowledgements

Giovanni Cecchetti, *Giovanni Verga* (Twayne, 1978)

DH Lawrence (ed Anthony Beal), *Selected Literary Criticism* (Heinemann, 1955).

La Lupa

(*The She Wolf*)

by

Giovanni Verga

a new version by

David Lan

from a literal translation by

Gwenda Pandolfi

Methuen Drama

Published by Methuen Drama

1 3 5 7 9 10 8 6 4 2

First published in Great Britain in 2000 by Methuen Publishing Limited

A CIP catalogue record is available from the British Library

ISBN 0 413 75450 2

Typeset by SX Composing DTP, Rayleigh, Essex
Printed and bound in Great Britain by
Cox & Wyman Ltd, Reading, Berkshire

La Lupa

This translation of *La Lupa* was first presented by the Citizens Theatre, Glasgow, in October 1995. The cast was as follows:

Pina	Yolanda Vasquez
Mara	Patti Clare
Nanni Lasca	Paul Albertson
Bruno	Matthew Zajac
Aunt Filomena	Irene Sunters
Janu	Bill McGuirk
Lia	Jill Peacock

This revised version was first presented by the Royal Shakespeare Company at The Other Place, Stratford-upon-Avon, 22 June 2000. The cast was as follows:

Pina	Brid Brennan
Grazia	Karen Bryson
Nanni Lasca	Declan Conlon
Mara	Mali Harries
Neli	David Mara
Malerba	Paul McEwan
Bruno	Tom Smith
Janu	Glynn Sweet
Lia	Emma Swinn
Aunt Filomena	Janet Whiteside

Director	Simona Gonella
Designer	Nicky Gillibrand
Environment Designer	David Fielding
Lighting Designer	Simon Kemp
Music	Mia Soteriou
Actors' Trainer	Roberto Romei
Sound	Andrea J. Cox
Music Director	Michael Tubbs
Assistant Director	Emma Wolukau-Wanambwa
Production Manager	Mark Graham
Costume Supervisor	Claire Murphy
Company voice work	Andrew Wade and Neil Swain
Stage Manager	Maggie Mackay
Deputy Stage Manager	Paul Sawtell
Assistant Stage Manager	Robin Longley

La Lupa

Characters

Pina, *called La Lupa – 'the she wolf'. She's thirty-five but still beautiful and provocative. She has the firm breasts of a virgin, luminous eyes set in dark sockets and a mouth like a flower in the warmth of her pale face.*

Mara, *her daughter. Delicate and sad. It seems as though someone else's guilt weighs heavily on her fair head. She's afraid to look directly at anyone with her timid eyes.*

Nanni Lasca, *a good-looking young man. He likes women but even more he likes himself. Sober and hard-working, he wants to get on in the world. He has a long narrow forehead, wiry hair, the teeth of a wolf and the eyes of a hunting dog.*

Bruno, *a light-hearted boy who accepts whatever luck brings him, including the odd girl or two on the threshing floor.*

Neli, *yellow and gaunt, weakened by malaria. He drops down in a corner exhausted at the end of every working day.*

Janu, *the boss. As serious and dignified as you'd expect of one of his age and occupation. Faithful to the good old ways, he even wears his grey beard in two tufts at the top of his cheeks.*

Aunt Filomena, *a lively old woman, toughened by work. She speaks like an oracle and knows more than the boss.*

Grazia *is so flat-chested and bronzed by the sun, you'd take her for a boy but for the smile on her cool lips and her coal-black eyes.*

Lia *is so wasted by poverty, she seems without age or gender. Even so, she smiles on life and on love.*

Malerba, *the clown of the group. He has the face of a monkey and a malicious sneer.*

The play is set in the countryside and in a small town near Modica in southern Sicily in the second half of the nineteenth century.

Act One

A threshing floor.

Nightfall.

To the right, the hut where the harvesters sleep. To the left, a haystack. Heaps of maize and farm tools lie about.

In the distance is the wide sweep of the countryside, already deep in night's shadow. A river runs between rushes and marsh reeds.

From far away comes a mournful song. Bells tinkle as cattle go to drink. Dogs are heard barking all over the countryside. Blown by gusts of the sirocco, the ripe maize rustles. At moments of silence the murmur of water gets louder as does the incessant chirping of cicadas.

The moon rises, fiery red. It fades little by little in a sultry halo.

It is after dinner.

Bruno, Malerba, Neli, Grazia *and* **Lia** *sit listening to* **Aunt Filomena** *tell a story.* **Janu,** *the boss, stands at the entrance of the hut, smoking.* **Neli** *nibbles a piece of brown bread.*

Filomena   Now, what happened to the witch?

Janu *(each time the wind blows, he turns to look)*   Feel that? Like a fire burning the sky. Tomorrow we'll sweat.

Filomena   I'm telling a story.

Janu *(with a shrug)*   Get on with it.

Filomena   The witch went to live in an enchanted castle. All the bricks were made of gold, they were covered all over in jewels. She never put a foot out into the air, never. She stayed inside and, when a traveller passed by, she'd let him see her standing at a window. What could he do? With her beauty, she'd draw him in. Then the two of them, they would . . . you know what they'd do. Young, old, who could resist her? Not even the priests.

Bruno (*laughing*)   That's the bit I like.

Filomena   What would you have done? She was a witch! She was old but she made herself young, fresh and sweet as a girl of fifteen. Her eyes shone like two stars.

Malerba   That's my girl! Where do I find her?

Filomena   In hell! Shall I tell you what she did with those fools when she'd squeezed them dry? A tap of her wand – pouf! They're donkeys. Another tap – pouf! They're pigs. Then one day a holy man, a saint, happens to hear what's going on. 'I'd better see for myself,' he says, 'or the whole world will go up in smoke.'

Malerba   He wanted to have a turn himself, that's all he wanted.

Filomena   You say that about a saint? That's it. Not another word from me.

Malerba   Who cares? Her stories, do you think they're true? She sucks them out of her thumb, makes them up as she goes along.

Filomena   Maybe I do and maybe not. One thing I can tell you: in the time of my stories, men were men. They were decent and God-fearing and good.

Bruno   I believe you. It's all true, every word. (*To* **Grazia**.) When I look into your eyes I know there are witches in the world. (*He blows her a kiss with his fingers.*)

Janu (*gravely, taking his pipe from his mouth*)   Witches or no witches, you know the saying:

'Woman is kindling, man's the spark.
Along comes the devil and he blows.'

Bruno (*to the girls, pretending to kiss them*)   You blow to me, I blow to you . . . Look at the kindling now, as true as God.

Grazia (*pushing him off with a laugh*)   Keep your hands to yourself. I don't want them.

Malerba (*suddenly leaping up*)   It's that witch. She's scratched us, we've got an itch. We want to jump up and leap about.

Bruno (*to* **Neli**)   Put your arse over your toes and play us a tune.

Malerba (*to* **Neli**)   Come on!

Neli   Jump up, leap about? What do you think I've done all day? Sat on a stone waiting for a job?

Janu   I gave you a job.

Neli   You did!

Janu   I pay you for a day's work, yes or no? I feed you, I give you straw to sleep on, yes or no?

Neli   You pay me, you feed me but my bones feel like broken stones. Jump up, leap about?

Bruno   Lazy bastard. On your feet! Up, up!

Malerba (*to* **Neli**)   Give us a fast one. And don't ask the boss to pay you for it, do it for love. (*To* **Grazia**.) On your toes! (*To* **Lia**.) Up, lazy bones. Here we go!

Neli *has taken his instrument from his saddlebag. He sways awkwardly as he plays, leaning on one foot then the other.*

Bruno (*calling towards the back*)   Pina! What the hell are you doing all this time?

Malerba (*to* **Grazia** *and* **Lia**)   You need persuading? Why? Take a tip from Pina. No one needs to persuade her. Wherever she goes, everyone's dancing, everyone's happy.

Bruno (*calling*)   Does it take so long to wash your face? Come to me, my beautiful Pina!

Nanni Lasca *comes on. He has a pitchfork over his shoulder. He pushes it into the haystack.*

Nanni (*joking*)   Hey! Are you calling the wolf? Don't. She'll run in and gobble you up.

Bruno   What have you been doing to her?

Nanni   Me? Nothing.

Bruno   Where is she?

Nanni   How do I know? I don't keep her tied to my belt.

Filomena (*smiling*)   No, that's her bad luck.

Nanni   I've got other things on my mind. All day the harvest, then the sun goes down, all the animals, I have to feed them . . .

Malerba (*his hands to his mouth, calling*)   Pina, my sweetheart! Pina, my darling! Feed us! Pina feeds everyone!

Janu   You're spiteful! Bite your tongue! Bite it!

Malerba   She *is* my darling, boss, and she's your darling, she's everyone's darling! Hey, hey, he's playing, no one's dancing. (*To* **Filomena**.) It's up to us.

He dances in front of her, inviting her to join him.

On your feet! Show the girls how you danced when you were their age!

Filomena (*leaping up*)   When I was young we said:

'Afraid to dance?
You're not worth a glance.'

She dances with **Malerba**.

Look! I've worn well, no? A little oil on my joints is all I need.

They dance. When **Malerba** *stops,* **Filomena** *dances in front of* **Janu**, *inviting him to dance with her.*

Bruno (*to* **Janu**)   Boss! Your turn! Bring oil for his joints!

Janu   We're squeaky old machines, are we?

Filomena   Strong machines!

Janu   That's more like it.

Grazia (*encouraging him, merrily*)

  'Afraid to dance?
  You're not worth a glance.'

Janu   Why shouldn't I if I feel like it?

Standing opposite **Filomena**, *he rocks clumsily to and fro. When she sits down, he goes to invite* **Grazia** *in the same way.*

Janu   Your turn, little wagtail.

Grazia *dances with him. When he sits, she dances in front of* **Bruno**, *inviting him. He leaps lightly round in a circle, snapping his fingers and shouting.*

Nanni (*laughing*)   Oh, oh, oh! That's the only work you do well. Pity you can't make any money out of it.

Bruno   Who wants money? I dance because I love it! Hey! Hey!

When **Grazia** *has danced enough, she sits with* **Filomena**. **Bruno** *invites* **Lia** *to dance by jigging up and down and shouting out in front of her.*

Nanni (*lying on the straw*)   He's got taste, that boy. Enjoy yourselves, both of you!

Malerba (*pushing in front of* **Bruno**, *pulling him by the arm*) My turn! Give someone else a go!

Bruno (*breaking free*)   Go to hell! I'm dancing! Hey! Hey!

Pina comes on, a bundle of maize on her head. She throws it down in a corner and comes forward smiling and tidying her headscarf. **Malerba** *runs to her with open arms.*

Malerba   My darling, my sweet! Dance with me. Come! We'll make the earth tremble.

Pina (*laughing*)   No, no . . . I'd rather dance with him. (*She curtsies flirtatiously to* **Nanni**.) If I deserve such an honour.

Malerba   It has to be him, huh, only him? Well, that's not news. Much good you get out of it.

Pina (*scornfully*).   Someone spoke to you?

Malerba (*to **Nanni**, teasing*)   She wants you! Can't you hear? Has your ear gone deaf?

Bruno (*laughing*)   That boy sees nothing, hears nothing . . .

Pina (*sings gently, teasingly, to **Nanni**, moving to and fro in front of him*)

'You who have eyes and do not see,
    Oh, why were those eyes given to thee?'

Bruno (*to **Nanni***)   Get up! Lazy bastard!

Nanni (*grumbling*)   Dance if you have the strength. Me? The whole day, my blade in my hand, cutting, slicing. I had just enough strength to eat. What must I do now, dance all night? I can't.

Janu (*laughing, to **Pina***)   That boy, I know his type. He'll do nothing to help anybody.

Pina (*flirting wth **Nanni***)   I say:

'If a man says no to me
    It's 'cos I'm too good for him, you see.'

*She invites **Bruno** by dancing gracefully opposite him, stretching out her apron with the tips of her fingers, tilting her head on her shoulder.*

Bruno (*excited*)   Forget him. When I'm with you I feel . . . what? Like a lion! Even if I were dead in my coffin, you come near – watch out!

Malerba (*to **Pina**, excited by her dancing*)   Save some for me, just a scrap. Ah, ah. Chains couldn't hold me!

'If a man says no to me
    It's 'cos I'm too good for him, you see.'

So why throw yourself away on that animal? (*Indicating **Nanni**.*)

Grazia (*laughing, to* **Nanni**)

'Afraid to dance?
You're not worth a glance.'

At last **Nanni** *catches fire. He gets up with an awkward smile.*

Nanni   All right! Fine! If that's what you think of me . . .
Here I am, I'm ready.

Pina

'Arrive late,
Nothing's left on the plate.'

With a laugh she turns her back on him and joins the other women.

Nanni (*stung*)   You've stoked me up. Now I'm a volcano.
I'm going to blow!

Mara *comes on with a bundle of maize on her head. As she lays it
down with her mother's,* **Nanni** *goes to meet her.*

Nanni   I was ready to dance, your mother turned me
down. You dance with me. (*To* **Neli**.) A fast one! I like my
shirt drenched in sweat.

Mara (*drawing back timidly*)   I don't.

Nanni   You too?

Mara   Forgive me.

Nanni   What's wrong with me?

Mara (*even more shyly*)   Nothing. I never dance.

Nanni   But why not? Are your legs too weak? Is your
heart too hard?

Mara (*lowering her head, blushing*)   No . . . Thank you . . .
I can't . . . Forgive me . . .

Nanni (*hurt, but singing playfully*)

'Heart of rock, heart of stone,
Will you leave me all alone?'

Malerba (*teasing, to* **Nanni**)   Leave her. You want her
mother to scratch her eyes out?

Pina (*roughly, to* **Malerba**)   Stop it! Leave my daughter
in peace!

Malerba   What did I do wrong? Did I hurt her? (*Pushing*
Nanni *jokingly.*) Leave her daughter in peace!

Nanni (*laughing*)   So that's the game? (*He gives* **Neli** *a shove.*)
Leave her daughter in peace!

Neli (*almost falling, angrily*)   What's it to me? (*He shoves*
Bruno.) Leave her daughter in peace!

Bruno   My turn, is it? (*He lunges at* **Grazia**.) I pass it on to
you, sweetheart! Leave her daughter in peace!

Grazia *leaps away laughing, then dodges* **Malerba** *who tries to
push her from the other side.*

Grazia   I don't like this game.

Lia *also moves out of the way.* **Malerba**, *pretending to have lost his
balance, staggers at* **Pina** *with open arms.*

Malerba (*of* **Pina**)   Her turn. She loves it . . . Leave her
daughter –

Pina (*fending him off, scornfully*)   Keep your hands to
yourself, you.

Malerba   Why? Are they dirty? I have to wash my hands
for you? Since when?

Pina   They're as filthy as your tongue.

Malerba   Suddenly she's delicate. Breathe on her, a
bruise. Has the devil become a saint in her old age?

Pina   You're an animal! Dirty! Disgusting!

Malerba   You're right, that's what I am, an animal.
Good, I won't touch you. (*To* **Nanni**.) You touch her. Your
hands are pure as snow.

Nanni (*laughing, to* **Pina**)   Ignore him. It's the wine talking.

Pina   What talks in you? Vinegar?

Nanni   Why do you say that? What have I said to you?

Pina (*sadly*)   Nothing . . . Let it go . . . Forget it . . .
(*Changing her tone, sweet but still sad.*) I brought you some
cherries from the vineyard. I don't care, be as sour as you
like. I climbed up and picked them for you. (*She offers them to
him in her apron.*) Do you want them or not?

Nanni   If you want me to have them . . .

Bruno   Quick to take, him, always.

Nanni (*to* **Bruno**, *then* **Malerba**)   Have some, all
of you . . .

Pina (*throwing the cherries into the air*)   There're plenty!
Enough for everyone! Eat!

Nanni (*surprised*)   But why are you doing this?

Pina (*her eyes brimming with tears*)   I could ask the same of
you. 'Why are you doing it?' (*Suddenly angry, she turns her back
on him.*)

Neli (*on all fours, looking for cherries*)   It's a sin to waste them.
They're a gift from God.

Malerba (*waving his hands for silence*)   Shh! Shh!

Janu   What now?

The sound of dogs barking.

Malerba (*roaring with laughter*)   The dogs! The dogs! Our
noise has driven them crazy!

Janu   They'll feel my stick! So will you!

Malerba   They're calling to the moon!

Bruno   The dogs and the lovers. (*To* **Grazia**, *romantically.*)
Who are you thinking of, this second?

Grazia (*coquettishly*)   No one.

Lia   Nor me.

Malerba (*to* **Pina**)   Speak to the moon. She's your friend. Don't you tell her when you're unhappy?

Nanni (*singing playfully*)

'I'm unhappy. Why complain?
No one cares about my pain.'

Pina (*bitterly, to* **Nanni**)   The moon's up there for everyone . . .

Malerba (*to* **Mara**)   Then, Mara, you tell us if she won't. Who were *you* thinking of?

Nanni (*smiling at* **Mara**)   You don't dance, you don't talk. What do you do?

Mara (*ignoring him, to* **Pina**)   Shall I fetch water from the river?

Pina (*roughly*)   Yes, go. Go, get out of here! I don't want to see you.

Nanni (*to* **Mara**)   Why do you put up with her?

Mara   What can I do?

Nanni   You're not a child. You could get married . . .

Mara   I don't want to.

She turns her back on him and goes into the hut.

Malerba (*shouting after* **Mara**)   Better hurry or your mother'll beat you to it.

Pina (*annoyed*)   Why don't you mind your own business?

Malerba   Oh, you, what you want you get. You're better than your daughter and you know it. You weren't born to be a widow . . .

Pina (*threatening*)   You looking for trouble? My teeth are sharp. I use them.

Malerba   I know you do. You chew men up – skin, bones
. . . Lord, protect us from those teeth of yours.

Bruno   Liar! You'd die to have her chew you up.

Malerba   And you? And him? (*Indicating* **Nanni**.) He's
first in line with his hands pure as snow.

Nanni (*laughing*)   Me, no, I've got thick skin. I take a lot
of chewing.

Pina (*to* **Malerba**)   And what your wife gets up to, do you
know as much about that?

Malerba   Listen! You hear? The wolf's howling!

Janu   Stop it, all of you! If you can't pass the time nicely,
go away, go somewhere else.

Nanni (*moving closer to* **Pina**)   What does his wife get up to?
Tell us.

Pina (*angrily*)   Nothing. Like me. I get up to nothing. But
you're so sour with me, you with your thick skin. Your
heart's even thicker!

Nanni (*turning away from her, singing*)

  'Heart of rock, heart of stone . . .'

Bruno (*to* **Grazia**, *romantically*)

  'Heart of stone, heart so hard,
  You who forget me and no longer love me . . .'

Grazia (*smiling, also romantically*)

  'Oh, girls, girls, haven't we heard
  Of lies concealed with a sugary word?'

Juno   That's good! That's what I like! Now everyone has
to sing one.

Nanni (*to* **Neli**)   You start.

Neli   Someone else go first.

Malerba   I will!

Filomena   Hold your tongue! We know your songs.
There are young girls.

Bruno (*to* **Lia**)   Then you.

Lia (*shyly*)   I don't know any.

Grazia   Nor me.

Bruno (*to* **Pina**)   Then you!

Pina   No.

Grazia   You know hundreds.

Nanni   She wants us to beg her.

Pina (*flashing a glance at him, then lowering her head*)   Good,
I'll do the first that comes into my head. (*She sings softly, as if
to herself, with her elbows on her knees and her head in her hands.*)

> 'Gorgeous carnation, my darling, my sweet,
> How can I love you, oh, how?
> You found my heart where it lay in the street.
> I've come to fetch it back now.
> Many hard hearts have grown soft in my arms.
> Yours is the one that I long for.
> The only hard heart who won't fall for my charms
> Is the one I've sung this song for.'

Bruno   Where did that come from? Wonderful. She's
a devil, that woman.

Malerba (*to* **Nanni**)   Your turn, you gorgeous carnation.

Nanni (*laughing awkwardly*)   Me? What do I know about
songs? I'm an animal.

Malerba   If she sings, you must. If you don't, you *are* an
animal with stones in your ears.

Lia   Now *he* wants us to beg him.

Nanni *gets to his feet, half laughing, half annoyed. His gaze doesn't
settle on anyone. He clumsily beats out the rhythm with his finger.*

Nanni

'Don't speak unless you're spoken to.
How you sow you'll reap.
Don't bite off more than you can chew.
Look before you leap.'

Malerba (*to* **Pina**, *laughing and wiping his mouth with his hand*)
Did you hear what he said? So you can give up hoping.
He feels it very deeply.

Pina *leaps up in a fury and throws a bowl at him.*

Pina   How deeply do you feel that?

Malerba   Ah! Damn wolf! She can use her claws! (*He flings himself at her.*)

Janu   Stop it! That's enough! Stop it!

A brawl, everyone shouting. The men try to hold **Malerba** *back, the women grab* **Pina**.

Neli (*getting clear of the others*)   This is how it always ends, everyone bashing each other, like in the puppet show!

Mara *runs on from the hut.*

Mara (*frightened, almost weeping, to* **Pina**)   Mother, what's happening?

Nanni (*to* **Malerba**)   Leave her alone! Why do you taunt her, pick on her, poke at her?

Malerba (*still annoyed*)   Why do you defend her? Because she wants to eat you, the wolf?

Pina (*shaking her fist at* **Malerba**)   I'll show you why you're right to call me wolf!

Janu   Hey! Hey! You've drunk too much, the wine's gone to your heads. But we know how to deal with this. There's a way to settle everything. (*To* **Pina**.) Go down to the river. Now! Fetch water for all of us. (*To the rest.*)   That'll cool her blood.

Pina (*going to get a jug, still threatening* **Malerba**)   You'll make me curse Christ, you.

Mara (*to* **Pina**)   Don't, I beg you.

Pina (*to* **Malerba**)   Watch out!

She goes off with the jug.

Malerba   Damn wolf! She spits at me, all of us. Why? Because she can't get it out of her, what she feels for him! (*Indicating* **Nanni**.) She's bursting with it.

Janu (*pushing him out*)   Worry about the animals, that's enough for you. Have they eaten? Go make sure. Give them fresh hay before you sleep. Do you hear what I'm telling you?

Malerba   I hear you, I hear you. But why hire a woman like that? There are hundreds all wanting work. Women like her come looking for one thing, trouble! And lovers . . . And with those words, my friends – good night.

He goes.

Mara *has stayed to one side, wiping her eyes on her apron.*

Nanni (*to* **Mara**)   Forget him. You know what he is, an animal.

Mara   But why do they always argue with her?

Nanni   He makes a lot of noise. Don't listen.

Mara   Would you like it if I said those things about your mother?

Nanni   You're angry with me?

Mara   Not with you. With my life . . .

Nanni   Your life's not so bad. You know what they say:

'From the thorn so sharp
Comes the rose so sweet.'

Mara (*bitterly*)   Ah, you're like everyone else. Leave me, leave me . . .

She turns her back and goes into the hut.

Nanni   Fine, I'll leave you. Why shouldn't I?

Filomena (*to* **Grazia** *and* **Lia**)   Let's go. It's late. The sun gets up early . . .

Bruno (*pretending to go with them*)   Here I am. Off we go, girls . . .

Lia (*running off, laughing*)   Jesus and Mary!

Grazia (*pushing him off*)   Get thee behind me, Satan!

Filomena (*brandishing a pitchfork*)   See this? This is all you get!

She goes into the hut with **Grazia** *and* **Lia**.

Janu (*to* **Bruno**)   To bed! Off you go!

Bruno *goes out.*

Janu   Who's watching the sheep?

Neli (*collecting his things*)   I am.

Janu   So why're you still here? Lying about's all you're good for. Watch out! Let the sheep in here on to the threshing floor, I'll break your head!

Neli   Boss, how can I watch all of them all night long? If they warned me: hey, mister, we're going here, we're going there . . .

Janu   Lazy piece of –

Neli   No, boss. Don't call me lazy.

Janu   Get out! Unless you want to feel my boot.

Nanni   I'll guard the floor. Go, go. I'll do it. I'll sleep out here.

Neli *goes out.*

Janu You'll do it? Good. Keep your eyes peeled, you hear me? Good man. Good night.

He goes out.

Nanni (*arranging his things for sleep*) Good night. Sleep well. God is watching.

Neli *is heard singing in the distance.*

Neli

'Along the silent road
To find my girl I go . . .'

Nanni *echoes the song as he spreads hay under his knapsack to make a bed.*

Nanni

'My girl, I love her so . . .'

He sits on his bed, stretches out his arms.

And tomorrow will be the same as today.

From the fields comes the sound of dry leaves rustling.

Nanni Who's there? A wild beast? An evil spirit?

Pina *comes on carrying a jug of water.*

Nanni You. (*Laughing.*) You gave me a fright.

Pina *sets the jug down near the door of the hut.*

Pina (*frowning*) You and your jokes. Whatever happens, you make a joke of it . . .

Nanni Still angry? The river didn't cool your blood?

After a moment she goes to him as if she's made up her mind. But her arms hang down in a gesture of despair . . .

Pina What have you got against me? How have I ever hurt you?

Nanni Me? Why? What did I say?

Pina *sinks down wearily. She speaks as though to herself, mournfully.*

Pina   If I've hurt anyone it's me. To you I've done nothing. And nothing to that animal. So why does he curse me? And with you hearing every word . . .

Nanni   He fools around, that's how he is. Forget him. Good night.

Pina   Good night to you, to anyone who can sleep . . .

Nanni *(still in a mocking tone)*   You can't?

Pina   Me? Never. As you know.

Nanni   Get someone to sing you a lullaby. I'm dropping off . . .

Pina *(after a silence)*   You are as you are. And I bless the saint who made you that way.

Nanni *(laughing)*   That way? Which way?

Pina   You pretend. You have eyes, do you really not see? No, you pretend.

Nanni   In the dark no one can see.

Pina   It's better in the dark. In the dark, words don't lose their way. They go straight to the heart. Yours cut me deeper than a knife.

Nanni   I don't understand. Is that a riddle? I'm no good at working out riddles.

Pina   Oh, your head, what a head you have, hard like your heart, hard as a stone.

Nanni *(almost wailing)*   I don't understand what you're saying. I can't make any sense of it!

Pina   Listen. Someone's dying right in front of you, do you ignore them? Do you turn your head away?

Nanni   Dying? Why're you talking about dying?

After a silence **Pina** *sings, her elbows on her knees, her chin between her hands, almost suffocating with pain.*

Pina

> 'Gorgeous carnation, my darling, my sweet,
> How can I love you, oh, how?
> You found my heart where it lay in the street.
> I've come to fetch it back –'

Nanni   Is that the only song you know?

Pina (*drying her eyes, feverishly*)   It's always in my mouth . . .
My heart's so full . . . You say you don't understand, you
pretend not to see me roasting on the fire . . . They call me
the wolf. But you, you're the wolf. Why? You like to watch
people die right in front of you . . .

Nanni   For God's sake, what do you want?

Pina (*bending over him, her face against his, snarling like a wild
animal*)   You.

Nanni (*exploding with laughter*)   Me? No. Give me your
daughter, not you. Give me your daughter with her soft,
sweet flesh . . .

Pina   Oh . . . I want to see your eyes weep like mine.

Nanni   Forgive me. I was joking. You know the song:

> 'Boys, time flows like water
> So leave mother hen and screw her daughter.'

Pina   You joke about that too? It's fun for you, is it, to
trample on my face, on my eyes? Why not, I'm the wolf,
isn't that what they say? I talk to you, I like to be with you
so I'm a wolf, I'm filth. When you've used me up, throw me
away like a rag.

Nanni   No . . . Listen. This is what I believe.

> 'Don't bite off more than you can chew.
> Look before you leap.'

Pina (*bitterly*)   How sensible you are. You never do a thing without having a good long think about it.

Nanni   I *have* to think about what I do. Who am I? Nobody. Where do I work? A day here, a day there . . . If I let myself get tangled up with you where'll it end? In what kind of trouble?

Pina (*humbly*)   What trouble could I cause you?

Nanni   Every kind. I'd never be free of you, never. I have to sort out my life . . . time to get married . . . and so on. You understand? All I've got in the world is my name and my health, that's it. I have to think about . . . putting together enough to offer to some woman. You, for example. Would you give your daughter to a man who was tangled up with someone like you? Don't be offended . . .

Pina (*mortified*)   Offended? I'm not . . . Nothing *you* say offends me . . .

Nanni   Look, that's enough. It's late. Good night. I mean it this time.

He turns his back and lies on his bed. After a moment **Pina** *speaks, her head in her hands, almost moaning.*

Pina   You'd do even this to me, put the knife in the hand of my own daughter?

Nanni   Let me sleep!

Pina (*hoarse and stuttering*)   So I guessed it. You want my daughter? Take her.

Nanni (*surprised, turning to her*)   What the . . . ? Do you mean that?

Pina   Yes, I mean it.

Nanni (*amazed*)   You'd give her to me as my wife?

Pina (*nods a few times before she can speak*)   What you want, can I refuse? You want my daughter, take her. Me, I'll go away . . . far away . . . where I'll never see you . . .

Nanni *looks hard at her, then turns his back as if he thinks she wasn't serious.*

Nanni   Good. We'll discuss it some other time.

Pina   No! Now! It's what you want, so let's sort it out right away.

Nanni (*leaping up*)   You're really serious?

Pina   *I* don't make jokes about things like this.

Nanni (*overjoyed*)   Well! So! Jesus. If you mean it, I'll do it. Yes! Right away.

   'Afraid to dance?
   No one gives you a glance.'

That's the truth.

Pina (*sinking down*)

   'No one gives you a glance.'

Nanni   So, Sunday, we go to the priest, sign papers, do everything that has to be done. You know I have nothing?

Pina   What do you want me to say to you?

Nanni   Everyone knows I'm honest, I'm healthy but money – not a cent. You'll give your daughter whatever you have?

Pina   I'll give her everything – my house, my clothes. What you want, I'll do. To me nothing matters. I'll find a corner, lie down, I'll die . . . far from where you can see me . . .

Nanni   No, you'll stay in your own house, why shouldn't you?

Pina   My house? What do I care . . . ? My life's over.

Nanni   So all we have to do is ask your daughter. Maybe she'll have other ideas.

Pina (*with tears in her eyes*)   My daughter . . . my flesh and blood? She'll want you, don't worry, she'll want you. Mara!

Nanni   Now? You want to do it now? In the morning. What's the hurry?

Pina   If the tooth aches, pull it out.

Nanni   Yes, but even so . . . Tomorrow . . .

Pina   Can you sleep with this thorn in your flesh? Can I?

Nanni   Do whatever you think.

Pina (*pushing him away*)   Go, go, get out of here! Leave me alone with her. This is between her and me. (*Calling.*) Mara! She's coming. You see? I call, she comes at once. Get away from here!

Nanni *goes off.*

Mara *comes sleepily out of the hut, pulling her clothes straight.*

Mara   What do you want?

Pina (*struggling to keep her voice steady*)   I . . . He . . . Nanni . . . He's opened his heart to me . . He says he wants to marry you.

Mara (*astonished*)   Me?

Pina   You! Don't pretend to be a fool. He wants you. I said yes. Now you have to say if it's what you want . . .

Mara   What I want?

Pina (*swallowing her bitterness*)   He's chosen you, so you have to say yes or no.

Mara   What do you want me to say? It's so sudden . . . I didn't expect . . . I hardly know him . . .

Pina   He's been working on this farm a month and you don't know him?

Mara (*bewildered, stammering*)   I never thought about it, I swear. About him? I didn't!

Pina   Well, *he's* thought. And he's said what he wants. He's there in the shadows, waiting for your answer.

Mara (*strongly*)   No! Tell him no!

Pina   Because?

Mara   I'm not getting married . . . I don't want to . . .

Pina   What do you want, to become a nun?

Mara   I don't want to get married! I don't want that man . . .

Pina (*threatening*)   Tell me the reason.

Mara (*trembling*)   Because . . . how can I . . . ? You know better than I the reason . . .

Pina (*about to strike her*)   What are you saying? Speak clearly, very clearly.

Mara (*bursting into tears*)   Have I hurt you, Mother? How? Why do you want to hurt me?

Pina   You want me to beg you, Mara, do you? Yes, that would be beautiful, beautiful . . .

Mara   Let me go! In God's name! Tell him, you, this marriage, no, never!

Pina   But I told him yes. I've already said yes. And you'll say yes. Why? Because I want you to.

Mara   You want me to?

Pina   I'm your mother. I tell you who to marry, I choose your husband for you, isn't that so? (*Proudly.*) So I give him to you. Take him.

Mara (*her hands clasped*)   No, please, don't do this.

Pina   If I have to drag you to the church by your pigtails!

Mara   Don't do this! God will punish us!

Pina (*pulling her by her hair*)   Why do you say that? Why should he punish us? Speak clearly, very clearly!

Mara (*shrieking*)   Don't make me! Don't do this!

Nanni *comes on.*

Nanni   No, no . . . This is wrong. Do it nicely or don't do it at all.

Pina (*to* **Mara**)   Get out of here. (*To* **Nanni**.) You want to come between a mother and her daughter? You're that brave, that strong? (*To* **Mara**.) I said go! You want me to damn my soul for ever?

Weeping, **Mara** *goes back into the hut.*

Nanni   What happened? She said no?

Slowly **Pina** *regains control of herself. She smiles bitterly.*

Pina   Don't be afraid. It's me who's got the hard task now. Me.

Nanni   What's going on? You're smiling and crying . . .

Pina   What I did, you don't know what it cost me.

Nanni   Forgive me. Honestly, I'm sorry. But to break your back over this, no. If it works out, fine, I'm happy.

Pina   Leave me.

Nanni   But if no, too bad and thanks for trying to help.

Pina   Go away! (*She bursts into tears, covers her face with her hands.*) It's my heart overflowing. If you knew what's inside me . . .

Nanni   Listen. I feel bad. Is it my fault, this? Is it something I said? I only meant it as a joke . . . (*Embarrassed but with affection.*) Turn off the tap now, for God's sake . . .

Pina (*desolate*)   I can't . . .

Nanni   Try.

Pina   No. I did everything you wanted . . . I can't do any more. Oh, what you made me do . . .

Nanni   Me? I made you do what? I did nothing.

Pina (*her eyes blazing, filled with tears*)   At least now you know how much I love you.

Nanni   Yes, I know. I'm not blind, my heart's not made of stone. To give me your daughter and everything you own . . . What more can anyone do?

Pina   Nothing.

Nanni   Your heart's as big as the sea. To give everything, your house, your sheets to your daughter . . .

Pina (*covering her eyes with her apron*)   That's nothing . . . nothing . . .

Nanni   Nothing to you, maybe, but it's a wonderful thing. To give everything away . . . and you still a young woman . . . still good-looking . . . even more than your daughter . . . (*Teasing, to calm her down.*) It'll be nice for us, won't it, when we're related? (*Embarrassed.*) Come on, stop it . . . I don't know what else to say . . . You know what an idiot I am . . . can't put more than two words together . . . Hey, you'll make me do something stupid . . . (*Laughing awkwardly.*) Make me forget God . . . that we're going to be related . . . I'm not joking now. You're the devil in flesh, in bone, you are . . . Dry your eyes . . . do it! For my sake . . .

Pina   You know what you did to me? You put a knife in my hand. You said: slice out your heart, slice it out!

Nanni (*utterly lost*)   That's enough, you hear? To see you so upset, it's like a storm blowing through me. Stop it . . . if you love me . . . (*He embraces her.*)

Pina (*springing away from him, trembling*)   Don't dare touch me!

They stare at each other, both very pale.

Nanni   Why? Why?

Pina (*in a hollow, broken voice*)   You're vile. You're wicked.
You want me to go crazy.

Nanni (*half fleeing from her*)   No! Oh God! What do you
want from me?

Pina (*taking him by the arm*)   Shh! They'll hear us . . .

Nanni (*trying to pull away*)   No . . . (*His hand trembling, he takes
from inside his shirt an image of the Madonna.*) Devil, I drive you
out!

Pina   You think that'll help? It's useless. Throw it away.
How many times have I asked her to help me drive you out?

Nanni   We'll go to hell, straight to hell . . .

An owl hoots.

Nanni   Did you hear? It's bad luck! (*He shakes his fist at the
heavens.*) Burn in hell, devil animal!

Pina   That's me. That's me you're cursing. I don't care.
I've been in hell right here, right where we are. I've paid
already for what I'm going to do.

Nanni (*defeated, his legs shaking, his face contorted, without the
strength to resist*)   I'm damned . . . I'm . . .

Pina (*pulling him by the arm, her head bent, fierce and strong as a
wolf*)   Shh! Don't curse. Just come.

They disappear out the back.
Far away: the murmur of the river.
The rustling of maize.
The chirping of crickets.
Dogs bark mournfully.
The owl hoots again.

Act Two

A courtyard in a village.

To the right, a door and a window under an arbour. Below the arbour is a stone bench. To the left, a well and a woodshed. The wall at the back, topped with weeds and broken glass, has a door which gives on to the street.

In the distance, the village can be seen all the way to the Mount of Capuchins. On its left we see a corner of a monastery and a high stone cross in front of a church.

On the other side of the street, windows and balconies are decorated with paper lanterns and brightly coloured banners.

From time to time we hear the sound of a band playing in the square.

Mara *is decorating the house with myrtle twigs and coloured paper lanterns.*

Nanni *enters through the door in the back wall. He goes to* **Mara** *and embraces her.*

Mara (*surprised but happy*)   Ah! Ah! That's lovely . . . (*Suddenly shy.*) No, what are you doing? The neighbours can see us!

Nanni   Where's my son? Bring him here. I want to give him a big kiss too.

Mara (*after a moment*)   You've been to confession?

Nanni   You can tell?

Mara (*smiling*)   And this is the penance he gave you?

Nanni   No! No, this is no penance. I'm happy, can't you see? So happy! Fetch the boy. Call him. Where is he?

Mara   Wait. First tell me, what did you confess to?

Nanni   Aha! So I have to make my confession to you as well?

Mara   You don't want to tell me? Why?

Nanni (*embracing her again*)   Never mind all that. Nothing matters except I love you. And, oh, you deserve to be loved.

Mara (*her eyes gleaming with gratitude*)   Is that true? Is it? Tell me. Really, truly, you do love me?

Nanni   Fool, silly fool . . . How can I help it? Of course I do.

Mara (*almost crying with happiness*)   I believe you. Now, at last I do, I do. From the look on your face I know it's true. (*kissing his hand.*)   Bless you. What a wonderful gift this is.

Nanni (*also moved*)   What gift? That's enough, silly fool! Stop it now.

Mara (*her heart overflowing*)   No, I want to tell you. Now I can. Listen to me. You've made me suffer. You have. You've caused me so much pain. And sometimes I think you didn't even realise when you were doing it.

Nanni (*uneasy*)   Doing what?

Mara (*putting a hand over his mouth*)   Don't talk about it. And don't make me talk about it . . . (*Looking at him lovingly.*) Because now . . . you love me, only me? Is it true?

Nanni   Mara . . .

Mara   No, don't get angry . . . (*Smiling.*) I'm going to make a confession to you. At first, in the beginning I . . . I didn't want you, you know that . . . There was something in my head, dark and ugly . . . (*With a rush of tenderness.*) But now, no. You're the father of my child, our boy, and the new one. You're all I have, all I want. Yes, enough, enough, I know, we won't say any more. I don't have to now God has shown me his goodness . . .

Nanni (*moved but uneasy*)   Good, fine, very good . . .

Mara (*kissing both his hands*) All I want is to thank you. (*She puts her hands together and raises her face to the sky.*) Thank you, God, thank you. (*She weeps into her apron.*)

Nanni Are you finished? And what were you saying exactly? That you're happy, is that it?

Mara (*drying her eyes*) Yes! So I'll light these lamps for the saints with my heart singing! All the tears I cried in secret I'll pour like oil into these lamps.

She goes back to hanging the lamps in the window. **Nanni** *helps her. He speaks with the same religious fervour as she used.*

Nanni Glory to God! This year he'll be good to us, he'll give us the best harvest we ever had! He will, I know it. Our fields will be like paradise! Call our child, fetch him. I want him here, now, with us. Let him feel what I feel. Where is he?

Mara (*placing flowers in the window*) Wait . . . Let me finish this . . . I left him across the road with the neighbours. They're getting him dressed for the procession. All in white! He'll walk along with all the angels, in his hand a basket of white flowers. There, finished. I'll fetch him. His pure, white soul . . . That's why God's blessed me, for his sake . . . I'll call him.

Lia *comes in through the door.*

Lia Mara, hurry. They're just putting on his costume. (*Looking round.*) Oh! It's so beautiful. It doesn't feel like I'm in the village. It's like I'm back in the fields. No, in a garden. (*Calling through the door.*) Come and see what they've done to their courtyard! Come, come!

Grazia *comes in and looks round admiringly.*

Grazia Beautiful! Gorgeous! But the mayor's house, have you seen what they did there? And the square, it's completely green! Green, green. People are pouring in from all over just to look at it.

Nanni   So, everyone's happy. The harvest will be the best we ever had, thanks to God.

The sound of children passing in the street singing the litany. **Lia** *goes to see.*

Lia   It's the little daughters of Mary! Come and see. Beautiful! Angels! They're running to join the procession.

Grazia (*at the door*)   Look! There's Carolina. The way she behaves, oh, she's wicked, that one!

Mara   No! No longer, she's changed, she's repented. The Madonna opened her eyes!

Nanni   She's repented? Her? I'm glad to hear it.

Neli *comes in from the street.*

Neli   I'm sent by the boss. He wants me to tell you . . . (*His mouth open, he looks round*). Oh, oh! What have you done here?

Nanni   We did what we could, with our whole heart.

Neli   It makes my heart . . . Good. He sent me to tell you . . . In the procession, the banner of the farm workers, he wants you to carry it.

Mara   Ah! You see!

Nanni (*astonished but overjoyed*)   Me? Are you sure?

Mara   When things start to go well . . .

Nanni   Fine, if that's what he says. He's the boss. Here I am, I'm ready! Look, the palm of my hand, the banner, I'll carry it there.

Grazia   Look at him. His chest, suddenly it's twice as big.

Nanni   Don't tease me . . . For me it's an honour.

Mara   And the one who's been honoured is mine! My husband! Mine!

Neli   It's because you set everyone a good example, the boss says. Who put the idea in his head, huh? Your priest.

Nanni   I set a good example. Here I am, I'm ready. What do you need? My hands, my feet – whatever is needed I'll give.

Mara   I also want to confess to that holy man. I'll do it tomorrow.

Nanni (*moved, smiling*)   What have you got to confess? Even I could absolve you.

Lia   Everyone wants to be absolved. So what do they do? Money, money, people are spending and spending. On flowers, on flags, on new clothes. All year round they sin and sin again . . . Then comes a day like today . . .

Neli (*to* **Nanni**)   You've spent more money than anyone. Lamps! So many! You know how much oil they drink?

Mara   If we run out, I'll drain more from my eyes. God has shown me his goodness. You remember when Nanni was very nearly dying . . . Have you forgotten? His foot was almost through the last door. The house was black with mourning. I made a vow.

Nanni   Don't go on . . . You made a vow to the saints, keep it. That's all.

Mara   But that's all over, thank God. My husband has ended my suffering. Why? For the sake of our child . . . We must pray for him . . . We must pray with deep feeling!

Nanni   Where is he? I want to see my son dressed as an angel!

Mara   Yes, come, let's go, quickly, now, before they start the procession.

She runs out gaily, followed by **Grazia** *and* **Lia**.

Neli   So, what do I tell him? It's yes?

Nanni   Yes! How many times do you want me to say it? Yes!

Neli   Good!

Nanni Yes!

Neli Excellent!

Nanni Yes!

Neli Wonderful!

He goes towards the door.

Nanni Wait! Tell the boss, the crown of thorns for my head . . . I want them to be real! I don't want to pretend, I want them to hurt! Christ will be there! He'll be dead but he'll be there!

Neli If that's what you want, good.

Nanni I want it because it's right. We're sinners asking for forgiveness, yes or no?

Neli Whatever you say. I'll go and tell him.

He goes out. He comes back with a look of astonishment of his face.

Nanni What is it? Tell me.

Pina *comes in timidly, with a humble smile.*

Pina Happy Easter. I came to wish you happy Easter, all of you. So much time has gone by. I haven't seen you, any of you.

Neli And the crown of thorns? Must I tell him?

Nanni How many times . . . ?

Neli But now you have visitors. Will you still carry the banner?

Nanni Yes! Tell him!

Neli *goes.* **Pina** *has remained shyly in a corner.*

Pina I've been ill . . . It's rained so much, so heavily . . . I had a fever . . . But everything else is fine, thank God. The wheat is already so high.

Nanni And the vines?

Pina (*more confident*)   The vines? Already putting out shoots, strong ones as long as, oh . . . that long. I thought, well, you two, you don't bother to come and see us on the farm so I'll bring you the news. (*She senses* **Nanni**'s *unease and loses confidence.*) And also I came to say . . . I need help. The weeds, can I pull them all out by myself? Look at my fingers, look at them.

Nanni   You could have sent a message.

Pina (*mortified*)   You're angry because I came?

Nanni   No. But if you're here who's guarding the house?

Pina   A neighbour keeps her eye on it, and on the farm. There's no danger. From who? Everyone's come to the village. (*She looks round.*) You've done a great deal . . .

Nanni   All right. If you're here you're here.

Pina (*timidly*)   If I've made you unhappy, I'll turn round, I'll go back . . .

Nanni   When did you care what makes me unhappy . . . ?

Pina (*groping for words*)   I wanted to see you . . . to know how you are . . . Don't you care how I am? (*As though her heart were broken.*) I could die out there, no one would know . . . or give a damn.

Nanni   All right! We'll tell Mara you've come to see the doctor.

Pina   Mara? What does she care about me?

Nanni   Don't say that. She cares about you.

Suddenly it's as though **Pina**'s *legs can't support her. She sits under the arbour and looks away so she can dry her eyes without being seen.*

Pina   What am I? I'm a dog. Alone. Without a master.

Nanni   Can't you keep your mouth shut? If you're found here . . . if people see you with me . . . then I will wish you hadn't come.

Pina (*turning her tear-filled eyes to him*)   Why? What do
I do wrong?

Nanni (*afraid to look at her, he pretends to be busy*)   You do
nothing . . .

Pina   I do nothing. I want nothing.

Very agitated, **Nanni** *looks at her in silence, then goes to her and
speaks in a low voice.*

Nanni   Listen . . . Today I went to confession. I've put
myself in a state of grace before God.

Pina (*lowering her head and opening her arms submissively*)   Well,
that's good for you . . . But something's frightening you.
What?

Nanni   I'm afraid of the effect on Mara . . . if she finds
you here.

Pina   Why shouldn't I be here? It's Easter! Everyone's
here!

Nanni   You know why it's wrong! And so does she!

Pina *turns away from him. She puts her shawl back on and makes for
the door.*

From outside comes the sound of a crowd.

Nanni (*stopping her*)   Wait. The neighbours have seen you.
You'll make things worse. (*He runs to the door, pulls it open and
calls to people passing by.*) Hey! You! Come in here! Come and
see who's paying us a visit!

Bruno *comes in.*

Bruno   Who is it? (*Seeing* **Pina**, *surprised.*) Oh! Forgive
me . . . (*He starts to go.*)

Nanni   You animal! I said come in!

Bruno (*looking suspiciously from* **Nanni** *to* **Pina**)   An animal?
Well, today's a good day to be an animal.

Voices (*from outside*)   The angels! Here come the angels!

Filomena *comes in. She sees* **Pina**.

Filomena (*scandalised*)   And you don't even close the door!

Grazia *comes in.*

Grazia (*to* **Nanni**)   The angels are outside. Aren't you coming? (*She sees* **Pina**.) Oh! (*Coldly*.) How are you?

Pina (*humbly*)   Thank you. Fine. And you?

Grazia (*to* **Nanni**, *embarrassed*)   Your wife sent me to fetch you . . . I'll tell her she'll have to wait . . .

She turns to go.

Nanni   Don't go!

Grazia   Forgive me, I'm in a hurry.

She goes out quickly.

Filomena   There's a story. A man was filled up this high with sin, and all his sins were against who? Jesus. So when he went to settle his accounts before God, what he found written in God's book . . . No, I'll say nothing. And on Good Friday! God wrote in the book: 'How many nails have you driven into my son's flesh? Do you have to add another?' And with that I greet you and leave you.

She goes out. **Bruno** *follows.*

Nanni   You see? That's how they'll all be.

Pina *doesn't move.*

Nanni   Nothing to say?

Pina (*with tears in her eyes*)   What can I say?

Pina (*whispering, with his fist almost in her face*)   I can say plenty. I was ill, very ill. My foot was almost through the last door. Even then would the priest come near me? No. I've looked at death with these eyes!

Pina (*retreating, trembling*)   What do you want me to do?

Nanni   Why did you have to come? Why today?

Pina   But what have I done wrong?

Nanni   I went to confession. I see you, what's it worth?
Nothing.

Pina (*anguished, suffocated with tears*)   And what have you
done to me? Do I complain? People see me, I'm talking,
laughing . . . What's in my heart, who sees that? No one . . .

Nanni   I see it. That's the worst part. So does Mara. If
you knew what she looks like. Skin and bone. What does she
say? Not a word. But inside, its teeth gnaw. It's eating her
up. Every night I hear weeping . . . because of who? You!
I'd rather she took a knife and stuck in here, here, here . . .
When she looks at me with those eyes, with that silence . . .

Pina (*not looking at him*)   At me too she looks with those eyes
. . . the moment I get here . . . (*Her voice hoarse.*) Me, who
made your bed for you, the two of you, on your first night,
with my own hands . . .

Mara *rushes in.*

Mara (*furious*)   So it's true!

Pina   Yes, I'm here. Yes, I came to see you . . . to see
how you . . .

With tears in her eyes, **Mara** *bends to kiss her hand.*

Mara   Well, you see how we are . . . We're very well.
(*To* **Nanni**, *angrily.*) So this is why you didn't come to see
your child, your angel. You've missed him now. He's joined
the procession.

Pina   It's my fault. Blame me.

Nanni   No, no, you've done nothing wrong.

Mara   He's right. You've done nothing wrong. Why
shouldn't you come here? You own this house, after all.

An embarrassed silence.

Pina   Oh, and the vineyard, it needs hoeing. You see? That's the news I came to tell you.

Nanni   Fine. We'll do it. We'll come and hoe the vineyard on Monday.

Mara   So you've come here to take him away?

Pina   Can I do everything with one pair of hands? The grass is that high. If it rains there'll be weeds, weeds everywhere.

Mara (*bursting with bitterness*)   Well, now it's raining and hailing in this house too.

Pina   Does that refer to me?

Nanni   No, no . . . what she means –

Pina   I sweat blood on your land! In the rain, in the wind . . . And when I'm too tired to do more I go on and on . . . The bread I eat I earn.

Mara *weeps, holding her apron to her eyes.*

Nanni (*to* **Pina**)   You see? You see?

Mara   Let me weep. What can I say to her? Nothing.

Pina   Sometimes to say nothing is to scream.

Nanni (*to* **Mara**)   Come to the vineyard with me. You can help also . . .

Mara   With what? (*She points to her pregnant stomach.*) Can I hoe like this . . . ? With God's punishment inside me?

Pina   God's punishment, you call it?

Mara   Yes, His punishment, I do. Is that wrong? You always tell me I'm wrong. Maybe God's wrong. Or you are! You made this marriage!

Pina   And this is how you thank me? This warm welcome you give me?

Mara (*her eyes burning*)   What do you want me to do? Laugh and sing while they carry Christ's body through the village?

Nanni   Stop it! I'll get rid of her. (*He takes* **Pina** *by the arm.*) Come and see your grandson.

Mara   No! Keep her away from my child! What has he done wrong? Nothing! Ever!

Pina   You're afraid? Of what? That I'll eat him up?

Mara   Why should you eat him? He's got your blood in his veins.

Pina   You think I'm a witch, is that it?

Nanni (*threatening* **Mara**)   Will you stop it! In the name of God!

Mara   Hit me, go on. If you think I've deserved it, here I am.

Pina   Sometimes words hurt more than blows. The words of a saint like you cut deeper than a knife.

Nanni (*about to burst, he restrains and crosses himself*)   Devil, get away from me!

Mara   Is that me? Or who? You want me to leave? Do you?

Nanni   No! I'm going! A mother and her daughter in the same house . . . This is hell! This is hell right here!

He storms out in a rage.

Mother and daughter look at each other in silence, pale and angry.

Pina   So, are you happy now?

Mara *glares at her.*

Pina   You make me feel like a beggar with my hand out to you and to him.

Mara *lowers her head.*

Pina   After you've taken everything I had . . .

Mara (*turning her back, her face in her hands*)   Leave me. I've had enough. Please.

Pina   Is that what you want, for me to leave you, never to see you, never to put my foot in your house, this house I gave you?

Mara   You gave it to me so I'd die here, so I'd waste away, so the light of my soul would go out . . . This house! You gave it to me so I'd damn myself in it!

Pina   I gave you everything! You took everything!

Mara (*turning to her, her voice quivering*)   Shut up! I don't want to hear!

Pina   Talk! Go on! Let the bile pour out of you!

Mara (*wandering about desperately*)   Oh God, oh Jesus, don't make me go on suffering and suffering . . .

Pina   You're suffering? Well, don't waste time on God and the saints. I've prayed to them over and over. Up there they've got better things to do than listen to our moaning.

Mara   You blame it all on the saints now, do you?

Pina   You see? You spit bile. I've noticed it for some time. There's poison in every word.

Mara   If there's poison in me, you put it there.

Pine   Then crush my head with your fists, do it, if I'm a snake. Do it! Then off you rush to confession, to get forgiveness.

Mara   Blasphemer! Devil!

Pina   Oh, stop shouting. No one wants to hear you.

Mara   Thief! You're a thief!

Pina   Shut up!

Mara   You've come to steal my happiness! You're a devil not a mother!

Pina (*like a wounded animal*)   Ah! You see how she is? You see?

Grazia *and* **Lia** *run in from the street.*

Grazia   What's happening? Is the house falling down?

Mara   Yes! It's fallen! It's in ruins! God has cursed it!

Lia   Mara, be careful what you say. People will laugh at you. Do you want that?

Pina   If you fall off a donkey, he kicks you. That's what they're doing to me, she and her husband.

Grazia   A fine time to discuss family affairs. The procession will come past any second.

Pina   I'm down so they kick me! I gave them everything! Now I'm taking food from their mouths, that's what they tell me!

Mara   Not just my food! She's drinking my blood.

Lia (*to* **Mara**)   You keep quiet, you first. You're her daughter.

Grazia   You want the whole village talking? Is that what you want?

Bruno *comes on.*

Bruno   They can hear you in the square. You're making more noise than the band. Everyone will think this is where it's happening, they'll leave the square and come here.

Pina   Let them come. Let them call the police. Let them tie me in chains.

Mara   It's your tongue they should tie up! And you too! They should tie you by the hair, there, over there in the square!

Lia   No, no, Mara! She's your mother!

Mara   What she says . . . it burns me . . . inside . . . burns
. . . here . . .

Grazia (*to* **Pina**)   Let's go. You've got more sense that she
has. Come. No more fighting today, agreed? Yes?

Pina   Why should I go with you? I'm in my own home.

Mara   Then stay! I'll go! I'll leave this damn house. It's
cursed! I'm leaving! For ever!

Pina (*threatening*)   Go before you drive me wild! Get out
of here!

Bruno (*coming between them*)   Hey! Hey! What are you
doing? What do you two think you're doing?

As they all shout and argue, **Nanni** *runs in.* **Filomena**,
Malerba *and* **Neli** *follow him.*

Furious, **Nanni** *hits out at both* **Mara** *and* **Pina**.

Nanni   One for you! One for you! They're talking about
me! Everyone! On every street! You can't stop? Here's
another! And for you!

Neli   It's goodbye to the banner.

Malerba (*waving his arms about, trying to make peace*)   The
band! Can you hear the band! It's coming! Here it comes!

The sound of the procession proceeding through the village.

Bruno (*to* **Nanni**)   Stop it! That's enough!

Malerba   What are you, Christians or Turks? Huh? Here
comes Christ's body. Are you Christians or Turks?

Filomena   Everyone's disgusted with you, the way you
carry on. It's shameful! Stop it! All of you!

Nanni   The whole village! Talk, talk! About me! You're
happy now, are you?

Pina's face is bleeding from **Nanni***'s blows.* **Grazia** *has been helping her wipe away the blood.*

Grazia   No, let me see. There's more.

Pina   It doesn't matter . . . It's nothing . . .

Malerba   To be kissed by an ox! That's what she likes, an ox's kisses!

Nanni (*pushing* **Malerba** *out*)   Get out! Go! Do you want a taste of this as well?

Grazia (*to* **Pina**)   Come, come, come, come with me . . .

She leads **Pina** *out.* **Lia** *and* **Filomena** *follow.*

Filomena (*turning back*)   Turks! That's what you are! Worse than Turks! God protect us and save us from the lot of you!

She goes out with **Bruno.** **Mara,** *weeping, is about to go.*

Mara (*to* **Nanni**)   Watch out! For what you've done to me, one day God will call you to account, then . . . !

Nanni   Stop it. You're the same as her. Both of you push my back against the wall . . .

Mara   How could you hit me in front of her? How can you give her so much pleasure?

Nanni   You, your mother, you'll make me do something insane, something terrible . . .

Mara   The two of you . . . Blasphemers! Criminals!

Nanni   Come now . . . Mara? Stop. For me . . . If you love me, if you do . . .

Mara   So that's why you kick me, tramp all over me. Because you know I love you? 'She loves me so I can do what I like with her.' I'll die! I'll die . . .

Nanni (*almost begging*)   Listen, Mara . . . Listen to me.

Mara   You know the state I'm in, and you find it in your soul to do this? When your son kisses your hand, can you look him in the eye? Can you?

Nanni   Please, don't you go for me as well. Every word you say is a knife in my heart. You want your mother out the way once and for all? I'll do it.

Mara   I don't believe you. I saw you, the two of you! The look on her face . . . On yours . . . Am I blind? Oh no, there's nothing between you . . . Then what did you go to confess?

Nanni (*tries to cover her mouth with his hands*)   Enough! That's enough, I said!

Janu *comes in.*

Janu   Animals! Worse than animals!

Nanni   It's them. It's not me. It's these women! They caused all this. They'll make me do something terrible!

Mara (*sobbing, to* **Janu**)   It's finished. I can't stay in this house.

Janu (*to* **Mara**)   Try to have a little sense, you at least.

Mara   I can't stay any longer. And I'm taking my son with me!

Nanni   Let her go. It's best. Let her.

Mara (*to* **Nanni**, *weeping at the door*)   Now your son has no father, no home . . . We'll live in the streets!

She goes.

Janu   If I had my way you'd be hanged.

Nanni   You're right. I deserve it.

Janu   You say this, you say that. You make promises. I believe you, you break them. With you, it's always the same thing.

Nanni   What promise have I broken? I've done nothing! Who says so? I'll rip out his tongue!

Janu   Then there'll be no one with a tongue in the whole village. Even your wife says so.

Nanni   She's crazy! She should be locked up! She gets an idea in her head, I don't know where it comes from . . .

Janu   Her idea is that you're an animal. She's right. What do we do with animals? Beat them.

Nanni   Try. I'd like to see you. But it's not me. It's *her*. I try to make her go away. My whole life I spend dodging and ducking and hiding to avoid her. I can't even go to the vineyard to do a little weeding . . .

Janu   Why? What are you afraid of if there's nothing between you?

Nanni   What am I afraid of . . .? Don't you know what she's like? If she wants you to damn your soul you do it, you just go ahead and do it . . .

Janu   You see what I'm saying? The way you talk about that woman . . .

Nanni   Oh Jesus! Sweet body of Jesus! What can I say to you! What can I do?

Janu   Speak to her simply and clearly. Say to her: 'Leave me alone.'

Nanni   How can I do that? This is her house. If she comes here, can I slam the door in her face?

Janu   Then go away. Leave this house. Either she must or you.

Nanni   Leave? And go where?

Janu   Away. To the fields.

Nanni   The fields? Easy to say. You understand nothing, nothing. Wherever I go, there she is buzzing round me. In

the hills, in the valleys . . . Oh no, away from here it's worse.
Buzzing around and around . . . She pretends she's looking
for herbs, wild herbs, in the forest. Like a wolf, she is. But
a wolf I can't shoot with my rifle . . .

Janu   Right. If that's how it is, this is what you do. Sell
everything you have, the lot. Leave this village, you and
your wife.

Nanni   I have nothing to sell. Everything belongs to Mara,
everything . . . She got it from her mother . . . (*Raving.*) I'm
chained hand and foot! Do you see? I'm tethered like a
horse! And to break a chain, the blow must be strong.

Pina *comes in.*

Nanni   Look at her. Do you see?

Janu   Shh! Shh!

Nanni   She's back. Look at her. She won't be happy 'til
I'm sitting in jail.

Janu   There'll be no jail and no more arguing. There's
a way to settle everything. (*To* **Pina**.) Do you know this
proverb?

> 'Mules and donkeys,
> Husbands and wives,
> Leave them in peace
> If they're to thrive.'

Pina   Am I disturbing someone? Who? What have
I done now?

Janu   What you've done . . . Nothing good, that's for sure.

Pina (*wiping her eyes, feverish*)   You know, boss, a mule, you
fall off, it kicks you. I'm poor, I'm crazy, they kick me.

Janu   You need a way to earn a living. We'll arrange it.
But you in one place, them somewhere else. The world is
big. And it's full of men.

Pina   You're right. And I deserve what you say.

Janu   What do people talk about? What others tell them. They like to chatter. We'll stop their tongues. Your son-in-law has been to confession. He's in a state of grace before God. Let him stay that way.

Nanni *and* **Pina** *stand with their heads bowed.*

Janu (*to* **Nanni**)   Have you understood me? Now I'll go and talk to your wife. I'll bring her home. (*To* **Pina**.) You've understood, I know you have. So do whatever you need to, then go to confession, then leave. Find your way to God's grace, if that's possible for you.

He goes.

Pina *speaks in a hollow, dark voice as though she were alone.*

Pina   No. It's not possible. A mother like me, who could I confess to?

Nanni   Then just go.

Pina   'Go.' 'Go.' Is that the only song you'll ever sing?

Nanni   I've sung it over and over. What good does it do?

Pina   If it doesn't do any good why sing it?

Nanni   Because I want to finish all this! Now! Once and for all! I want to climb out of this hell.

Pina   Hell? I thought you were in a state of grace. So do it. Climb out. What are you afraid of?

Nanni   Of you, the devil in flesh and in bone. You've put a curse on me. What are you on earth for? To damn me.

Pina *doesn't look at him. She draws water from the well and speaks in a hard voice.*

Pina   I came to town because it's Easter. I'm a Christian just as you are.

Nanni (*enraged, he grabs her arm*)   You? You?

Pina (*breaking free*)   Let me wash my face. No! This is my best dress. You'll tear it!

Nanni   Tear it? I'll tear you, right now!

Pina   Oh, you will? Me? You wouldn't know where to start!

Nanni   Blood of Jesus! Body of Jesus!

Pina (*fixing him with her gaze*)   Even now, even after all this time, you still don't know what a man is. All you know is how to drive people crazy, you. But to free a soul from torment with one blow of the fist, could you do that?

Nanni   Curse you! Damn you!

Pina   You're right. Don't think I don't know. Mothers like me? We should be burned alive. We should be fed to the pigs, mothers like me. And so should you. You keep me in hell, tied by my hair, like a madwoman! So you went to confession? So what? It means nothing. We're chained together, you and I, for eternity.

Nanni (*picking up an axe, brandishing it*)   I'll smash the chain!

Pina (*baring her breasts as though to challenge him*)   Do it! End it! With your own hands!

Nanni *pushes her behind the woodshed, his eyes wild with anger and horror, holding high the axe, screaming and foaming at the mouth.*

Nanni   Ah! Ah! What are you? The devil himself?

Printed in the USA
CPSIA information can be obtained
at www.ICGtesting.com
LVHW041102171024
794057LV00001B/217